PHANTOMS

BENJAMIN FORTIER

PHANTOMS

BENJAMIN FORTIER

Copyright © 2023 Benjamin Fortier

All rights reserved.
This book or any portion thereof
May not be used or reproduced in any fashion whatsoever
Without the permission of the publisher or the author
Except for the use of quotations

Publisher: Dead Reckoning Collective
Book Cover Artwork & Design: Andrew Doyle
Editor: Keith Walter Dow

Printed in the United States of America

ISBN-13: 979-8-9862724-5-0 (paperback)

DEDICATION

To the people who gave their bodies & minds in any of the numerous campaigns spawned by the attacks on September 11th, 2001.

To my family and the family of all service members, especially our Gold Star families.

To the creatives and contemporaries to my left and right—
I'm glad to be in this long race with you.

To the Marines, Sailors, Soldiers, and Airmen that held it down in the Sunni Triangle from 2004 - 2011.
This one is for you.

CONTENTS

The Men With Guns 13

Appreciation of the Marine Corps Infantry In Haiku Form . 15

In the Palace of Thieves 17

Lead the Way 19

Multi Domain Operations 21

Keep Them At Bay 23

The Grisly Truth 25

The Vortex Beckons Us 27

What Makes Us Do It? 29

Palm Springs - February, 2006 31

A Calling 33

Baby Mariam 35

The Night of the Long Day 37

Don't Inhale the Black Smoke 39

Bequeathing A Deadly AO 41

Among the Berserkers 43

Sipe 45

My Post-War Woman 47

Trembling Trigger Finger 49

In Pain 51

The Gnashing Gears of the War Machine 53

Anamorphic 55

Honed 57

Like Thunder Claps from the Mountains	59
Do Your Job	61
Hey There, Devildog…	63
Eat the Apple…	65
A Compassionate Killer	67
Cosgrove	69
Contact: The Valley of Debris	71
Haiku	73
Left of Bang	75
Right of Bang	77
What Makes Us Do It? (Part II)	79
What Happened to Us?	81
You're Gonna Have to Try Harder Than That	83
The Alienated	85
Far From Home	87
The Line of Departure	89
Climb to Glory	91
T-72	93
Herminator	95
Overwhelmed by Tragedy	97
Memories	99
Dust Off	101
26 August 2021	103
The Fire Inside	105
Find Your Way	107

APPRECIATE

The United States military holds the highest standards of any professional military in the world. It has faced major upheavals from within and without for more than two hundred years. Some of the finest Americans that ever lived have worn a uniform; they have sacrificed and bled in order to protect the formation of a more perfect union.

It is not uncommon for the everyday American to stand alongside their troops as they get sent off to faraway lands. They welcome broken combat veterans home from hellacious battlefields with hugs and handshakes, genuine reminders of what, and for whom they were fighting.

The US military has been there to distribute meals to starving families, protect the weak and defenseless from armed barbarians, and liberate the oppressed from tyrannical despots.

There are poems in this book that give praise to our military institutions. They salute the general officers and politicians that rightfully use our warriors as a tool for justice, peace, and stability. They honor the values of service, devotion, and moral courage in the face of adversity and brutality.

DEPRECIATE

Despite the professional nature of our all-volunteer military, it is not without its blemishes. Outside of the standard barbarism of ground warfare, our munitions and ordinance have poisoned battlefields for generations to come. From the abundant usage of Agent Orange in Vietnam to shelling with uranium-depleted rounds in Fallujah, our institutions have contaminated not only the local populations but our very own troops.

The citizens for which our military sacrifices so much are largely unaware of the hardships our service members endure. Unless they are an immediate family member or close friend, they are disconnected from the tours of duty, training evolutions, and unique stresses that come with life as a member of the armed forces, regardless of branch, job, or rank.

Corrupt leaders have used our firepower as a hock for their agendas. The military-industrial complex has deep roots in our society, and many tax-paying citizens are completely unaware of just how profoundly dependent many of our social systems are to this machine.

There are poems in this book that are meant to raise skepticism. They were written to question authority and explore uncomfortable truths about our status as "Demo-cracy's Vanguard." They shame the concepts of blind nation-alism, the glorification of violence, and the warmongers that put our country's bravest citizens in these predicaments.

THE MEN WITH GUNS

The vast desert is suddenly interrupted
By the sprawling cityscape.
An abrupt protrusion of four-story buildings,
Mosques, and water towers
Jutting up from beside the ancient Euphrates River.
This is a holy land to many. Historical to the rest of us.
Babylon.
       Mesopotamia.
              The Fertile Crescent.
                              Uruk.
Palm groves and bridges.
A highway with a cloverleaf interchange.
Busy storefronts and cluttered alleyways.
Familiar spectacles in this land so far from our place of
origin.

Three years prior,
The invasion sorted out the remarkable obstacles:
       Tanks.
       Scud missiles.
       Chemical agents
       To be used in fear
       By the deposed dictator.

Now, our obstacles are invisible and deadly,
With the ability to hide in plain sight
Or disappear back into the population we swore to protect.
Bombs buried in the broken pavement blow up
And break the backs of unsuspecting Marines and soldiers.
Sometimes they go off prematurely.
They wipe out youthful soccer games in the streets.
Tiny bodies scattered by the blast.
Their friends and loved ones carry them off

on gurneys

in agony,
As we taunt the assailants to come out and fight us—
       The men with guns.

APPRECIATION OF THE MARINE CORPS INFANTRY IN HAIKU FORM

0302 (Infantry Officer)
Leading from the front
Restrained war hounds on their leash
They sharpen the spear

0306 (Infantry Weapons Officer)
Chief with bursting bomb
Bona fide weapons guru
Proud title: Gunner

0311 (Rifleman)
Movement to contact
The harsher environments
Make them more vicious

0313 (Light Armored Reconnaissance)
Within the armor
They conduct reconnaissance
Bushmaster ready

0317 (Scout Sniper)
Long range surveillance
Patience, waiting for hours
Target marked—headshot

0321 (Reconnaissance)
Swift - moving by sea
Silent - undetected op
Deadly - suppressed shot

0331 (Machine Gunner)
Interlocking fields
Chattering guns, cyclic rate
Barrels briskly changed

0341 (Indirect Fire)
"Hanging on Gun Three!"
The mortar lingers, waiting
Raining steel and death

0351 (Assault)
Stacked on the door
The breaching charge is in place
Dynamic entry

0352 (TOW Missile Gunner)
Armor is in range
Wire-guided rockets launch
Metal on metal

0369 (Infantry Unit Leader)
Infantry Marine
Deemed by our congress to be
Mentors and leaders

0372 (Critical Skills Operator)
Elite warrior
Highly skilled, direct action
The Raiders return

IN THE PALACE OF THIEVES
Modified version from *The Silent Whispers of Omens*

Before us, the river of filth swelters
And snakes among the haven of bandits.
Bastard children who seem to have been
Forgotten by the essence of love.

Tribal wars rage under the fire
Of the glowing sun.
No guilt is felt as the martyrs
Pillage their castles built upon catacombs.

As we walk into the palace of thieves
The darkness around us breathes,
Wielding weapons and hatred
Unfathomable to my ignorance.

This place was once golden
And soaked with the glory of man.
It's where civilization took its first breath
Where humanity swelled inside its lungs.

But now I look around and realize
How corrupt divinity can become.
Black tar poured on to the golden idols,
Laced with the poison of hate.

This is a war-infested land
Where we must escape
       or die trying.
Who can save this hate riddled place?
Who can shift its nature?

LEAD THE WAY

Sweat lingers in the fabric
Adding grams of weight,
To the uniforms of the elite commandos.
They move in teams of two,
Silently approaching the target area.
The night envelops them,
Shrouding their outline.
Their heightened senses,
Feel the environment.

A break in the silence,
Feeding off violence.
As triggers click,
Enemy bodies fall
Slumped against the walls.

Moving with cunning
And confidence,
Slipping through the target area.
Gathering intelligence;
Pictures, documents, thumb drives and laptops.

Then disappearing
Back into the murky air,
Taken away by Chinooks,
Whose rotors chop away the clouds.
They ascend into the Heavens,
To return once again,
When the moon is full.

MULTI DOMAIN OPERATIONS
Previously Published in *War... &After: The Anthology of Poet Warriors Vol. 2*

The armies that will withstand the future must have
The capability and will
To dominate all facets of war.
While the peril of nuclear holocaust
Created a deep worry in state actors,
They found subversive tactics
That would fool the observers
And solidify their victory.
There is always a way around
The boundaries of legislation.
Instantaneous communication
Leads to belt fed propaganda machines
Spewing memes of divisive content
Controlled by the same state actors
That are claiming no offensive is currently ongoing.
While masked troops with rifles
And wheeled, armored vehicles with machine guns
Roll through the streets of some village.
News reports claim mercenaries while
Intelligence analysts believe their rivals
Are simply warming up the gears
Of their newly formed war machine.
Internet operations
Cyber-based warfare
Multi-faceted tactical scenarios
Winning battles without ever firing a shot.

KEEP THEM AT BAY

Intelligence gathering
Threat analysis
Clandestine operation
Learning their movements.

Reconnaissance
Sabotage
Hand drawn maps
Encrypted messages.

Evading the police
Working on theatrics
Blending into the crowd
Undetected by surveillance.

In order to keep
Our enemies at bay,
Good men and women
Must enter the fray.

THE GRISLY TRUTH
Previously Published in *War… &After: The Anthology of Poet Warriors Vol. 2*

A vicious fight ensues in a city halfway around the World.
A dilapidated building houses a gang of insurgents,
Taking on a team of heavily armed Marines.
Close quarters combat.
Rifles going off inches from their targets.
The fighters are racked with concussions.
Ears ringing. Adrenaline spiking. Hands shaking.
Engulfed by the fog of war, an American shoots his friend
In the back of the head.
A grenade goes off simultaneously
And the dead body shields his compatriots
From the thousands of pieces of searing hot shrapnel.
A lull in the fight allows the men to drag the fallen
Out of the kill zone.
There is no time for sorrow. The enemy is still in proximity.
Another several minutes are spent
Attempting to flush the insurgents
Out into the street
To be gunned down by a machine gun in a fixed position.
Finally, the rifles fall silent.
No one can understand how it came to this point.
Everyone is still in a state of shock,
Coated in a thin layer of dirt, sweat, and gore.
Lighters flick and cigarettes singe.
What lie could they possibly concoct
To make it seem like they didn't kill one of their own?

THE VORTEX BECKONS US

A chemical cocktail surges through the body
They make first contact with an unseen enemy.
They are focused, sharp, elated, and at peace.

Months of being on edge
They do not realize the mental fog has rolled in.
Their brains and bodies are tired and worn,
From the constant stress and lack of sleep.

Weary troops shoot at anything that moves.

The only remedy for the lives that were stolen,
Is aggressive, retaliatory violence.
This cycle of inhumanity takes its toll,
As a chemical cocktail surges through the body.

WHAT MAKES US DO IT?

The brain is revved to the red line
The unrelenting barking of the Drill Instructor
Keeps the atmosphere intense.
It is a simulation of battle.
We are at this depot to prepare our mind, body, and spirit
For a situation that will make this one look like anemic.

It all happened so quickly.
Basic training, Infantry School,
Then off on a deployment.
It was as if willpower took over and
Brought these goals to life,
Back to back
In quick succession.
Like the rapid fire of the machine guns
That would soon go off around us.

It was all so glorious
Yet terrifying.
The dichotomy of the human spirit
Is exhibited in full swing
On the front lines of war zones.

Maybe that's where the calling came from,
To be an observer of all that we are capable of.
All of the goodness, justice, and integrity
Contrasted with the chaotic apathy
And ruthless violence
Most of us are so unfamiliar with.

PALM SPRINGS - FEBRUARY, 2006

The last days in this cushy little country
Are spent comfortably numb
Wandering through the streets
In a drunken stupor.
Two hundred dollars worth of liquor is wasted.
We bought enough for forty people
And between three men
      We just can't finish it all.
What the hell were we thinking?

Reciting poetry and smoking cheap cigars and wondering.
Wondering. Wondering. Wondering.
What will the next few weeks dump on our laps?
Where will we be in the next few months?
Wrapped up in plastic or admitted to a hospital?
Laying down covering fire and tossing hand grenades?
Or bored out of our wits watching *Road Trip*
For the fourteenth time in a row?

These people all around us
Dumping their money into slot machines
And relaxing in the pool with their fancy, overpriced cocktails.
They had no idea where we were going
And I can't imagine they would care.

Wandering the streets alone and intoxicated
Hoping to get into a fist fight
So my first taste of uncontrolled violence
Wouldn't have to be in Iraq.

A CALLING

There was a calling that I heard as a young lad.
It was nurtured by mentors that embraced a spectrum
Of socially conservative ideologies.
Like their tutors before them,
They were disillusioned by the military-industrial complex
Into believing the cacophony that blared
From the defense cabinets
Since the end of the second World War.
Can't fault them for being so caught up in the noise.
Their experience in a uniform was pageantry at best.

Still, this calling fascinated my innate sense of adventure
And desire to help those less fortunate;
To embrace and defend the values and rights
That were inherited by me as a citizen
Of a free nation.
There was, however, an ominous side of that escapade
That I knew could alter the course of my life.
Violence and sadness blended to a degree
That an immature mind could not possibly fathom.
The possibility of physical and moral injury
Seemed plausible,
       But impractical.

In an effort to create a robust spirit
And a hardened body,
I began to expose myself to discomforts
That would have otherwise been avoided.
A physical fitness routine interrupted the desire
       To write poetry and play the guitar.
While my mind and body would thank me
For these endeavors,
The challenges became more disturbing.
The glorification of violence
       Was a sought after anesthetic.

Yet deep in the chambers of my being
        Violent conflict is deplorable.
I was injuring my sense of self before I even held a rifle,
Yet if I could not prepare the mind
To engage in the viciousness of a firefight,
Or to be subjected to the vehemence of war,
Hesitation on deployment
Could get me or my comrades killed.
This was an unacceptable outcome,
        So the desensitization campaign continued.

I had always admired the sacrifice of prior generations
And when the planes hit the towers,
I felt the calling beckon louder.
Honor, glory, and virtue
Are some of the first casualties on the field of battle,
Yet I was convinced that if I just believed a little harder,
        And prayed a little longer,
I could protect those ideals
        And bring peace to a land ravaged by war.

Instead, the man that returned home from conflict
Felt tossed over the coals by the military-industrial complex
Roasted on the spit until the tissue and skin split
To love and hate the calling,
It's where my feelings contradict.

BABY MARIAM

A city bombarded with uranium-depleted rounds
Injecting toxins into the soil
Of the once fertile crescent
Poisoning their limited water supply.
The dilapidated city will have life renewed,
But coalition forces still roam the streets
A year and a half after the major battle.

An IED ambush forces a platoon to dismount
And hunt for the trigger man.
A baby's cry catches the attention of the corpsman.
They lower their rifles to examine the child.
Bladder exstrophy—a rare condition
That will certainly kill her
If left untreated.

No formidable hospital within miles
Would be able to perform the lifesaving operation.
"We've got to get her out of here," the corpsman insisted.
Christopher Walsh
An EMT from St. Louis
Embedded with Weapons Company
As one of their medics.
Doc Walsh and his men would covertly
Enter Mariam's home
And provide treatment that warded off infections
Keeping her alive.

Weeks before the unit was slated to demobilize,
Walsh and two Marines were killed in their truck
Just blocks from the home of the Iraqi family,
But the rest of the platoon vowed to finish his work.
With time running out, Mariam was flown
To Mass General Hospital
For life-saving surgery.

A renewed chance at life
Thanks to the guardian angel
They called Doc Grumps.
As Christopher's mother
Stared into the eyes
Of the saved babe,
She could feel her son's presence
Like the warmth of
A shining light.

THE NIGHT OF THE LONG DAY

Between the casualty evacuations
Burnt bodies of our friends
Catastrophic vehicle kills
And a rocket hitting the hood
Of the skipper's vehicle
About ten meters in front of us,
The day had been long enough.
Five or so weeks to go until the steel hawks
Would lift us into the sky
And take us from the ever-present danger,
Hoisting us from the hell, we called home.

As if we hadn't been tested enough,
The movement back to the patrol base
Went from a ten minute journey
To an hour long ordeal,
Filled with more casualty evacuations
Burnt and dismembered bodies
Catastrophic vehicle kills
And panicked Marines
Unable to fathom the ambush we had stumbled into.

The day after,
While our two buddies were airlifted
To Germany to recover from their wounds,
I ignorantly volunteered to clean out
The back of the vehicle
From which they were evacuated.
> "I'm an eighteen year old PFC."
> "It has to be me."

Emotionally numb,
Climbing into the back of the green HMMWV
Where the mess of gore awaited.
Bits of bone
Congealed blood—
The aftermath of a hasty tourniquet
Placed above the knee
Of a mangled lower leg.

The pangs of that time
Reverberate throughout the duration
Of my life,
Like haunting echoes bouncing off
The wet walls of a dark cave.

A bright, sudden flash
Reminiscent of the one that filled
Our night vision goggles
On the night of the long day.
I awaken to my own screaming.
Fourteen years later
I'm home, but not alone—
The haunting echoes
Are creeping into my mind.

DON'T INHALE THE BLACK SMOKE

The lingering smell of burnt cordite
Wafts through the air on the wings of death.
The fire in the destroyed gun truck rages, and
The Marine with smoke-filled lungs wheezes.
Burning ammunition explodes,
We can't look away from this grisly sight
On this warm September night.

BEQUEATHING A DEADLY AO

We inherited a dangerous area of operations
Fifteen months after Phantom Fury,
When soldiers and Marines plowed
Through the ancient city.
Street by street, block by block,
Urban warfare not seen
Since the battles of Hue or Saigon.

The city consumed us,
In its quagmire of concrete
Black water, sewer streets,
Tire walls, garbage heaps.
Blue mosques and minarets,
Chanting out calls of death.

IED sweeps at zero four,
Red Bulls and Rip Its galore.
Drove over a hole with two 155s
Barely know how we made it out alive.
The trigger man tried to blow it.

And we thought that you should know,
We are bequeathing a deadly AO.
Insurgency activity has soared,
In case you thought you'd be bored.
"Have fun, we're going home."
In the streets of Fallujah, you will roam.

AMONG THE BERSERKERS

A writer in a war.
Capable of violence,
And all too aware
Of its dire consequences.

Among him stood the berserkers.
How they were ravenous with bloodlust.
Their hands mangled
From dozens of prior fistfights.
Their arms and shoulders bulked,
Ready to haul the massive weight
Of their heavy armaments.

He watched their rage.
How it would consume the battlefield.
Knocking down combatants
With well-placed shots
From a rifle
      Or a fist;
Laughing in the heat of the fight,
Unconcerned with their own well-being.

The writer felt the craze.
How it all changed
When a long day took a handful
Of their brothers away.
Firing his weapon blindly in anger,
As they covered a Marine crawling through
The puddle of fluids that soaked the highway;
A slurry of anti-freeze, diesel, and blood.

Even that night
The berserkers prayed,
To stack the bodies of their enemies,
And find a way out of that place.

SIPE

I learned of your death years after the fact
And it still came in like a freight train out of left field.
Not to say that we were particularly close,
But my mind immediately went to the image
I captured of you and another Marine
Relaxing outside our grueling training.
Laughing.
Smiling.
The way you'd want to be remembered.

As the sole keeper of the image,
It had to make its way
Back to your home,
To your family
So they can remember you
As the laughing,
Smiling man.

MY POST-WAR WOMAN

For months she watched me fall apart,
Clinging desperately to survivor's guilt.
As if it were a part of me.
As if it were my identity.

She moved on, and it made me realize
How glorious it was to be alive.
To feel those fears—to drain those tears
That my fallen brothers never could.

TREMBLING TRIGGER FINGER

The desire to follow a self-fulfilled prophecy
Of darkness and solitude
Pillars of strength are crumbling.
Liquor fueled bitterness brings out a guilty survivor,
    A young man struggling with his brush with fate.
"I'm breaking up with you."
    Her voice was stern as he refused and begged,
    But he could feel her resilience through the phone.
Her voice echoed in his mind.
It was the same night he sent his best friend
    Away to Iraq for the second or third time.

Trembling trigger finger
Tip toeing to the edge,
Peeking over the precipice to take in
The ungodly sights.
Voices taunt from the infinitely black whirlpool,
"Your friend is never coming back."
"You cannot be loved."
"You should have died in Iraq."
"You are better off dead."

Don't do it.

Don't fucking do it.
Or they'll be picking up pieces
Of your skull from your childhood home
For years.
You're not **ending** pain and suffering,
    You're **extending** it.
His hand lowers the pistol.
He looks himself in the mirror.
He wonders where to go from here.

IN PAIN

Did I make a difference,
Or just hurt people along the way?
A chaotic path
Of bitterness, trauma, and liquor.

Projecting my suffering
On anyone in proximity.
Letting them know
Our world is misery.

THE GNASHING GEARS OF THE WAR MACHINE

I went to war for the richest nation in the world.
Not because I had to,
But because I thought I should.

That impressionable teenager wanted to experience
The glory and heartache of a combat-tested infantryman,
But it's kind of gross to think about the luxuries
Afforded to us as an arm
Of the 21st century industrialized war machine;
Helicopters, tanks, close air support, and the advanced
Medical technology that only the richest nations in the world
Could dream of affording.
Our battle space had just as many coffee stands
As it did suicide bombers.
More people came in contact with STDs than the enemy
Gang bangs in trailers
While a General gave a rousing speech.
Chuck Norris demonstrating karate moves
USO sponsored cheerleader grooves
Country stars, models, comedians
Laughing about the state they were in.

But what about the millions of dollars in armaments
We left behind as the wars came to a close?
Did some accountant just chalk that up as a loss?
Fudged numbers that some mafioso bookkeeper
Would greatly approve of.
Who knows? I don't.
There's a lot of speculation,
Contemplation, and thought masturbation.
But at the end of it, we just can't get off.
We're left beating our meat until it's painful and raw.

Man, we were rich.
We had A/C, counter IED UAVs,
And that little dude who would bow to me
When he'd hand over my ice cream.
I'd feel kind of bad for the dogs out in the FOBs,
But at the end of the day, we just took what we were given,
Assignments and missions,
Someone else always had it worse, so buck up, buttercup.
Because back home,
Some coddler in the war machine needs to cash in.

ANAMORPHIC

Endless wandering.
The expenditure of energy is alarming.
Motivation wanes and primal instincts
Take control of the limbic system

Who is this person pulling the trigger?
Sprinting across a danger area
To dig into a harder piece of cover?
It is the animal within us
And it loves every second
Of this bloodlust.

It is the spirit that must come to grips
With the things it sees in war.
The animal will be sent back to its cage
Only to be fed scraps
Of leftover meat
But it never forgets the freshness
Of the blood from combat.

HONED

Vicious
Without being malicious.
Compartmentalize
Compassion
And violence.
Two storage areas
Of the spirit.

God merged with animal
Baring teeth.
Bringing fury
From beneath.
Primal instincts
Precisely honed.
Conducting warfare
Government owned.

LIKE THUNDERCLAPS FROM THE MOUNTAINS

Rolled down the embankment
The body lands with a splash,
Among the blood, mud, and corpses
Some face down—some torn apart.

The chatter of high-velocity machine guns
Matched with ferocious volleys of indirect fire.
Inside the minds of broken men
The incessant beating of a drum.

DO YOUR JOB

Don't ever think
I had it all together.
Despite some courage
And resilience,
I was scared and insecure.

But with fear comes focus.
With trust comes confidence.

When my peers realized
Job efficiency and teamwork
Were my priority,
They believed in me.

HEY THERE, DEVILDOG...

Hiding behind the stripes on your collar,
An institutionalized wiener—barely a scholar.
ASVAB waiver, recondo reject,
Hated by your troops who show you no respect.
Loathed by your peers, they know you're a turd,
You think you're a sheepdog, but you're part of the herd.

Incompetent at your job,
Incomprehensible on comms.
Sitting behind your desk,
While sending dick picks to our moms.
Unnecessary deflections corrections
On the gun line,
When you haven't touched a belt of ammo
Since 1999.

Of course we laugh at you behind your back.
You think we respect you because of your stack?
We're salty dogs too, and we know your kind.
All that gusto and glory takes place in your mind.

EAT THE APPLE...

There is a quote,
"Some people go their whole
Lifetime wondering if they made a difference;
Marines don't have that problem."

Thanks for the wisdom, Ron.
The difference I've made is not stunning
Nor worthy of history books
Nor valorous medals.

The difference was in my life's trajectory
Now embedded in lingering memories—
Echoes of laughter after nasty jokes;
Moments spent in awe of the firepower at our disposal;
An explosion and a flash;
Uncontrollable sobbing after a memorial ceremony;
Seeing a wounded Marine
Getting dragged across a street;
The dirt kicking up from an IED.

A lifetime of wonder.
It is not the intention in question
But the outcome of the consequences.
Ron, I did wonder if I made a difference
When Daesh stormed the walls at Baharia
And paraded their flags through streets
In which my brothers bled upon.

Don't give me this bullshit about
Rendezvousing in Hell—
We've been there.
We've seen it.
Hell is here.

We do wonder, Ron,
If the choices we made
Were careless, callous, or complacent.
We wonder about a lot of things,
And some of them
Seep into our nightmares.

A COMPASSIONATE KILLER

Running fingers over the essence,
Tracing the lines of experience
Coursing through this being.
Laughing at joyous memories,
Feeling the nature of divinity,
Recollecting moments of
Pure, unfiltered generosity.
Love, kindness, compassion
And violence.
Unfettered violence
The tracing fingers stop
      And remember.

A compassionate killer?
Shame is built up under Christian skin,
Attached to the bones
Calcified sin.
Toxic, burn pit fumes befoul the spirit,
Putrefying the marrow of being.

How the fuck can I be a loving,
Empathetic human,
And still hold on to the capacity to kill?
Will it outweigh my capability for love?
Or are these juxtapositions
Just two sides of the same coin?

The warrior in the garden,
Can turn a kama
Into a soul-reaping scythe.

COSGROVE

The earth shook
And we knew it was bad.
Upon exiting the darkened sleeping quarters
Our eyes, adjusting to the brilliance of the sun,
Noticed the sandy landscape jutting a plume of black smoke.
It was not supposed to be there.

A car bomb hit the Northern entry control point.
We were the closest unit to respond,
Cordoning off the area, watching panicked Marines & Iraqis
Run to and fro, as if moving their legs
Might bring someone back to life.

We were days away from wrapping up,
And the Marine that was killed was filling in for another.
Someone else's son got to go home
Because he stood watch.

And here we stood watch, looking over the
Scattered car parts mixed with melted asphalt.
Concrete barricades singed with debris.
The smell of burnt rubber,
Chemical residues, and destruction.
I saw the look on my friend's face
As he returned from the scene.
It was as if the Old Gods themselves escorted him
And toured him around the horror.

There was no reason to ask what he had witnessed
As he gently climbed into the passenger seat next to me.
I continued to stare at the burnt concrete barrier
Blocking the view of the carnage on the other side
Where the wretched horrors of war squirmed and mutated
Like a John Carpenter creature coming to life.

Months earlier, I might have been intrigued enough
To ogle over the grotesque vista,
But there was nothing more that I wanted than
To go home
And get away from the apathetic violence
That followed us wherever we went.
We were days away from leaving.
I wanted us all to return
With what sanity we had left.

CONTACT: THE VALLEY OF DEBRIS
Previously Published in *War… &After: The Anthology of Poet Warriors Vol. 2*

The endless miles of red sand
Kicked up in clouds as the convoy weaves
Its way through the Valley of Debris.
The spotter notices an unfamiliar object.
It wasn't there yesterday,
Or the day before.

Swerve, swerve.
The tires lose grip as the trucks lurch.
Throttles roar as the bomb explodes and
Tears off the rear quarter of the second vehicle.

Truck one stops hard,
The security team spills out.
Truck three is trapped.
The Commander is not a patient man.
No follow up. Eyes are wide open. Corners are scanned.
They feel the scopes of snipers on them.
The tow-bar is finally attached.
"What took so long?"
An annoyed voice comes over the radio.
They got lucky this time.

VEHEMENCE

I
Dogs of war await
Violent nature sustains
Success comes at cost

II
Insurgent pursued
Blending into the city
Running for his life

III
Blinding flash of light
This is no quiet evening
Rounds snap overhead

IV
Choking on your fear
Embracing this dance with death
Willpower exposed

V
First patrol outside
The wire which confines our pride
Courage is embraced

VI
Bloody high back floor
Wash away the grime and gore
More patrols in store

LEFT OF BANG

Eyes scanning

Rooftops
Treelines
Hands

Sudden movements are deadly
Hidden enemies await
Living life on edge
A distraction from fate

RIGHT OF BANG

Dust and debris fall upon us gently
"Is everyone okay?" I ask, heroically
As our brains were rattled by the IED

WHAT MAKES US DO IT? (PART II)

Driven by a sense of duty, a young man leaves behind
His eldest daughter. She is only nine years old.
He is convinced that God, King, and Country
Will greet him on the killing fields.
However, there is nothing but death, sorrow, and violence.
He never returns home to see his youngling grow up.

Driven by a sense of honor, a teenage boy leaves behind
His aging father.
He, too, was a veteran of a previous conflict.
The boy is convinced that shame will wash over him
If he does not follow in the path of his sire.
Even the might of a father's protection cannot save
A young boy from the ravages of a chemical attack.
The boy dies alone, and his body is never recovered.

Driven by the propaganda of a mighty,
Industrialized war machine,
Entire swaths of society stand behind the hawkish tactics
Of a ruthless, post-imperial nation
That skirts international laws and regulations.
The gullible are sucked into a convolution of misinformation,
And the skeptics are cast aside
As unpatriotic revolutionaries.
Belligerent nationalism is poisoning our values,
Especially when
It is intertwined with corporations and the economy.

WHAT HAPPENED TO US?

Hatred.
It lingers like smoke
Ceaselessly floating through a cigar bar,
Or like a tsunami of soot
Kicked up from an IED.

I carried it inside me,
In case of an emergency.
We fired weapons in hatred,
And it felt good to release
That negative energy.

We were weaving knots of war
Where malice begets malice.

Compassion.
Left alone in the street,
Shrouded by plumes of cordite,
Forgotten like a lost child.
As chaos erupts around her,
She clutches her companion:

    Hope.

She never lets it go.
We lock eyes,
And I remember what it was like
To be so young.

YOU'RE GONNA HAVE TO TRY HARDER THAN THAT

Baking heat
Summer sweat
Bitter sweet
Some regret

Leaving home
Feeling alone
Middle child
Barely grown

Some forgive
Some forget
Some get fierce
Becoming threats

Planting bombs
For us to hit
TBI
We still won't quit

THE ALIENATED

Feeling desperately disconnected
Rejected, ejected from a society
I felt I had protected.
Cold steel in the hands of a
Social deviant,
Yet, in the eyes of the citizens,
I'm a savior, not a miscreant.
A predator for profit
With no clear vision
Of reintegration
Back into the world
After this mission.

I'm excited while suppressed
And under fire,
But depressed when I'm home
And get called a liar
By some old timer that probably
Dodged conscription
When I volunteered for a war
That required a conservative subscription.
He did no favors
With his lies and boasting,
For when my tears came
I was the one roasting.
Self-loathing and disgust
Driven by bloodlust,
Aching to get violent
And wonder,
"Why am I trapped in this vortex?"

Change happens from within
And from without;
Self-realization
Is stronger than self-doubt.

FAR FROM HOME

Displays of horrific memories
Adorn the ancient cavern walls.
Pointy sticks become swords—
Swords become rifles.

A flash of flagrant aggression
In an attempt to shape our world
Boasting about conflicts they commenced,
As if they understood violence at its very core.
As if they could recreate the pulsating, beating heart
    That squirms in the jaws of the wolf.

What motivates a man to cut the throats of foes?
What drives a woman to hurl herself upon jagged stones?

Hesitant to take another's life
The grip of shame that comes with murder.

    "I feel nothing."

He lies to himself and his God.
The real world feels so far away.
He is far from home
In every way.

Benevolence is found in between the cracks of rifles,
Weeping as they drag away their dead,
Laughing as they gun down the enemy in close proximity.
Humanity's viciousness is proudly adorned,
    Juxtaposed by the shining love
    For their brothers.

THE LINE OF DEPARTURE

Bellying up to the loading berm.
Mag inserted; go condition one.
Wave to the gate guard.
The troubled kid

Kicked out of the platoon.
Prepare to pass over the line of departure.
A line that extends from the heart
To the trigger finger.

CLIMB TO GLORY

Those mountains in the distance;
They're nothing quite like
The ones back home.
Ridges of redemption,
Valleys of violence.
Dreading the ascension,
Adoring the silence.

T-72

Skeletal remains of the bear
That once tried to traverse the mountains
Come closer—see the graveyard.
Haunting lessons ignored not even twenty years later
By the next warmongering superpower.
Their bones bleached in the Kabul sun,
Never again to fire their main gun.

HERMINATOR

"Rank has its privileges."
Like front row parking at the drill center.
Like skating out of deployments and patrols.
Like avoiding NJPs and Page Elevens
That my boys got stomped with.

Your rockers don't mean shit
If you suck at leadership.

PHANTOMS

"Once we get out of here, things will be different."
How naive we were to believe that fairy tale.
So many of us would return home
Only to face the demons we hid away,
While dragging brothers off kill zones
Burying the bodies they departed.

The lurking monsters would manifest themselves
In addiction,
In violence,
In the inability to maintain stable relationships.
We turn the guns on ourselves
As we become overwhelmed
By the ineffable tragedies behind us.

MEMORIES

Their keepsake from home
A staunch reminder
That another world outside this one
Is empty and longing for our presence.
I watch them run their fingers over the sacred item
As if they're caressing the face of their loved one,
Reassuring them of the moment when they will return.

MEMORIES

DUST OFF

Nine line is initiated.
Blackhawk is in the sky.
Keep the pressure steady.
"We aren't gonna let you die!"

26 AUGUST 2021

Flooded by a profound sense of joy and sadness,
Emotional utilities we were unable to deploy
At the time of your loss.
Sudden, instantaneous violence,
Zipped you away from this existence.
In a flash of light, you were gone.

What we saw that day did not matter,
Not because you didn't care,
But because you simply were not there.
We remember you for who you were.
Are you alone in our memories?
Untouched by the hands of your lover,
Unaccompanied by your closest confidants.
Are you a prisoner inside our aging minds?

We are not captives,
Or stowaways of the flesh.
We are vessels of antiquity,
Children of divinity,
Brimming with intellect,
Capable of profound tranquility.
With more than enough room inside our hearts
For those that have passed along the way.
Despite our fragile, mortal world
Our spirits can't be kept away.

THE FIRE INSIDE

You are all that you have
And your roots grow deep
For in this indifferent world
You must strive to upkeep
Your body, your mind
And moral latitude
Through benevolence, benignity
And heartfelt gratitude

FIND YOUR WAY

How can those of us that have

Pushed the butterfly
Pulled the wounded
Punched PUCs
Plunged a blade
Dropped mortars
Stacked corpses
Counted their husks
Shot rockets
Saw the pink mist puff
Swept a leg
Watched death
Dodged bullets
Laughed at the violence
Cut someone down
Cracked a skull
Removed a limb
Rushed a fighter
Cried in mourning
Remembered their screams
Relived their deaths
Drank in sorrow
Lost all control
Put a gun to ourselves
Ran someone off the highway
Lied to our loved ones
Shouted at kids
Hurt our friends
Shoved a stranger
Gave a server an attitude
Went back on a promise
Rested on our laurels
Became complacent in our identity
Demanded undeserved respect…

Continue to contribute,
Continue to give back,
Continue to build a community?

Remember our burdens
Do not carry us—we carry them.

SITREP

I sit here at the end of August 2021 having witnessed from afar one of the greatest mass evacuations in recorded history: the extraction of hundreds of people from Kabul airport in Afghanistan. As we are subjected to witness yet another withdrawal, our exit from the Global War on Terror has felt about as awkward and foolish as our entrance.

A massive car bomb killed hundreds of people amidst the evacuation, including thirteen American service members. One of them was in their early thirties. Just like I am today. Another one of them was from Massachusetts, a place I too call home.

We must remember these people not as strangers, but as friends that we have yet to meet. I see pictures of these individuals assisting women and infants in the heart of the chaos at Kabul airport, and it reminds me that war exposes our human dualities in the most raw and extreme way. Despite the risk of extreme violence and trauma, there will always be individuals willing to suit up to be a killer one second and a nurse the next.

There will never be a moment where I don't think of combat. Its aura surrounds me everywhere I go. It seeps into the walls and through the plumbing and crawls deeply into my nose during the night. Even in the most tranquil moments of life, there is a searing heat from afar that reminds me of the sands of Iraq and the bustling markets of the Jolan District in Fallujah.

Granted, the majority of our deployment was rather uneventful. There were hundreds of hours of patrols where nothing ever happened. It was incredible to observe the culture and every day life of the Iraqi people. Their tenacity to carry on and provide for their family and community, despite the massive hardships they were facing, was awe-inspiring. The cultural anthropologist in me wanted to sit and hear their stories. Their resilience was unlike anything I could even fathom.

When we were attacked or were going on the offensive, that part of my brain became unplugged. The curious anthropologist shed their humanity, because if they didn't, they could become a liability in a gunfight. Depending on the circumstances, the artist, poet, anthropologist, musician, and emotionally intelligent human can remain unplugged for hours. Sometimes days or weeks.

Training helped. Being indoctrinated into a world-class military institution was definitely the right way to go to war. However, there was no training to plug back in. There were laughable attempts by psychiatrists, chaplains, VA health care members or Staff-NCOs to talk about trauma and dehumanization and grief, but most of the time it was a crock of shit; their approach was ineffective, they didn't seem genuine, or they were talking to the right crowd at the wrong time.

There was simply no way for me to fully process what we had just gone through via conventional means. Reverting to music and literature has given thousands of veterans a voice and a vessel to process their personal experiences as a war fighter and a human being. These platforms have always been there for me, and I knew I would be leaning on them outside the military. I severely underestimated just how necessary these activities would be for my mental, emotional, and spiritual well-being.

With that said, a part of me has been transferred to you. It's not quite as intimate as sex or violence, but I've given myself to these words. For my lyrics to arouse an emotional response in you is truly a humbling thing, and I thank you for allowing me into that space. This has been a piece nearly sixteen years in the works. The timing sure seems appropriate.

Stay creative. Stay compassionate. Be a warrior in a garden.

PREVIOUSLY PUBLISHED WORKS BY DEAD RECKONING COLLECTIVE:

FACT & MEMORY by: Tyler Carroll & Keith Dow
IN LOVE… &WAR: THE POET WARRIOR ANTHOLOGY VOL. 1
WAR… &AFTER: THE POET WARRIOR ANTHOLOGY VOL. 2
WAR{N}PIECES by: Leo Jenkins
LUCKY JOE by: Brian Kimber, Leo Jenkins, and David Rose
SOBER MAN'S THOUGHTS by: William Bolyard
KARMIC PURGATORY by: Keith Dow
WAR IS A RACKET by: Smedley Butler
THE FIRST MARAUDER by: Luke Ryan
WHERE THEY MEET by: Cokie
POPPIES by: Amy Sexauer
ROCK EATER by: Mason Rodrigue
REVISION OF A MAN by: Matt Smythe
ON ASSIMILATION by: Leo Jenkins
SANGIN, THEN AND NOW by Neville Johnson
A WORD LIKE GOD by Leo Jenkins

UPCOMING PUBLICATIONS BY DEAD RECKONING COLLECTIVE:

CARMEN ET ERROR by: Moises Machuca

DEAD RECKONING COLLECTIVE

Dead Reckoning Collective is a veteran owned and operated publishing company. Our mission encourages literacy as a component of a positive lifestyle. Although DRC only publishes the written work of military veterans, the intention of closing the divide between civilians and veterans is held in the highest regard. By sharing these stories it is our hope that we can help to clarify how veterans should be viewed by the public and how veterans should view themselves.

Visit us at:

deadreckoningco.com

 @deadreckoningcollective

 @deadreckoningco

 @DRCpublishing

FOLLOW BEN FORTIER

benjaminfortier.com

 @thebenfo

Photo credit: Emily Gehly

When he's not writing, BENJAMIN FORTIER enjoys spending time in the New England wilderness, creating music, watching hockey, tinkering with computers, volunteering with veteran organizations, and playing video games. He hopes to continue publishing, releasing music, and using his technology skills for the good of mankind—or until SkyNet becomes self-aware.

Phantoms is Fortier's third collection of poetry and his first published by Dead Reckoning Collective.

www.ingramcontent.com/pod-product-compliance
Lightning Source LLC
LaVergne TN
LVHW020935090426
835512LV00020B/3373